IMAGES OF S

Larkhall

Harry Dawson. This chap was a well-known character in Larkhall. Harry ran for miles around the area with his 'gird and cleik', until he was a grown man. Sadly, he was hit by a tram and later died. Harry was and still is today a legend in this area with many stories related of him – Larkhall was often referred to as Dawson's city. A 'gird and cleik' was a large metal ring with a long metal rod, the rod fitting into the groove in the inside of the round ring so that when you ran with it you could keep it turning.

IMAGES OF SCOTLAND

Larkhall

Helen Moir

NONSUCH

This book is dedicated to the memory of my mother Marion Perrie, who took so much pride in anything I ever achieved.

First published 1998
This new pocket edition 2006
Images unchanged from first edition

Nonsuch Publishing Limited
The Mill, Brimscombe Port,
Stroud, Gloucestershire, GL5 2QG
www.nonsuch-publishing.com

Nonsuch Publishing is an imprint of Tempus Publishing Group

British Library Cataloguing in Publication Data.
A catalogue record for this book is available from the British Library.

ISBN 1-84588-286-5

Contents

Acknowledgements

I would like to thank Mr Andrew Allan of the Wallace Hamilton Nursing Home in Blackwood, James Cunningham of the McWhirter Home for the Elderly, Andrew Cunningham, Miss Goodwin, James Grant, Revd James Hastie, William Holman, Alan and Jean Johnstone, Ian Kenny (Dial-A-Frame, Larkhall), Jim Laughlan, Larkhall Bowling Club, Larkhall Raploch Bowling Club, Larkhall and Hamilton Library, Larkhall Resource Centre, Guy Rodger, and St Mary's RC Church.

I would also like to give special thanks to Elizabeth Liouane, Iain Ferguson, and Bill Moir for his love and support.

Introduction

The town of Larkhall lies about seventeen miles east of Glasgow and has been the principal village for the Parish of Dalserf since the late seventeenth and early eighteenth centuries. The parish covers an area of approximately eleven square miles and includes Larkhall and the smaller settlements of Dalserf, such as Ashgill, Netherburn and what was once Millheugh. Larkhall sits on the west bank of the River Clyde, which forms the east and north-east boundaries of the parish. To the west and south-west runs the River Avon and the Cander Water.

The parish was originally known as Machanshire, probably from the Gaelic *maghan* (a little plain) and the Saxon *scir* or *shire* (a division). *Laverockha* which is Gaelic for a lark on the hill has been suggested as to how the name Larkhall was derived. The name *Levrokhall* appears on a 1773 map, and much earlier in a 1654 atlas, the name *Lakhouf* also makes an appearance as the site in and around the Old Cross. Houf was the old name for house, with Larkhouse possibly becoming Larkhall. To some of the locals, past and present, it has simply become known as 'Larkie'.

The early history of Larkhall is very non-descriptive but it seems that in the late fourteenth century it was made up of small farming hamlets with the name Machan. The lands, which were later to form the parish, were known as the lands of Machan (*Meeheyn*). These lands were to come under the auspices of the powerful Hamilton family, to whom the then parishioners would serve as serfs. The atlas of 1654 describes small farming settlements in what was to become Larkhall, with names like Raploch (*Roploch*), Millheugh (*Milheach*), *Skelliestoun*, *Struther*, and *Althoofm*. The spelling of Larkhall in this format did not come into common usage until the eighteenth century.

The Parish of Dalserf has a strong religious background and indeed Larkhall itself has a number of well-attended and thriving churches dating back to over two hundred years – St Machans in Church Street, Trinity church in Union Street, Chalmers church in Strutherhill, the Baptist church in Machan Road, the Congregational church in Machan Avenue and St Marys Roman Catholic church in Raploch Road.

The religious history of the parish goes back much further to Roman Scotland. The name Dalserf is thought to have come from St Serf, who is the main saint for the parish. The Dal is derived from the Gaelic *dail* meaning field or meadow, thus, Dalserf is the field of Serf. The mother church for the Parish of Dalserf, known affectionately as 'The Auld Grey Mother Kirk', stands in the picturesque village once known as *Dalserf Toun* and at one time was the main village for the parish. The village nestles by the River Clyde and the old church was built in 1655.

St Serf was an early saint associated with a number of Scottish places including Culross in Fife, but was also known to have worked in the Clyde Valley. The site of the Old Kirk at Dalserf is thought to be the location of St Serf's earliest church, although he is reputed to have ended his days at Dunning in AD 543. According to legend, St Serf ordained St Mungo (or Kentigern as he was also known) at Culross, and through him a long line of missionaries was created in the south of Scotland, which was often called the country's Cradle of Christianity. It is here that St Ninian and his disciples first preached and St Mungo founded his church. St Serf was a very well-educated and devout man. His mother was the daughter of Brudei, King of the Picts, while his father, the King of Canaan, was educated in Alexandria. He turned down the exalted office of Pope to follow his Christian teachings and left the land of his father to return to his mother's home in pagan Scotland.

The other saint associated with the Parish of Dalserf is St Machan, whose name is given to the area of Machanshire. Trained in Ireland in the sixth century by Cadoc Machan, Machan continued to work in the Clyde Valley, setting up what was probably his main centre at Dalserf. His name is commemorated in place names around the parish and particularly in Larkhall. Machan Brae, Machan Avenue, St Machans church and Machanhill Primary School are all contemporary examples.

The lands of Machan in the thirteenth century belonged to the Crown and formed the hunting ground of Cadzow. They seemed to have been possessed and repossessed during their history and also belonged to the ancient church of *Cadihou* (Cadzow). The lands came under the auspices of the powerful Comyn family and were Crown lands during the reign of John Balliol (1292-1296). After the coronation of King Robert the Bruce, who dispossessed the lands of Machan from the Comyn family by force, the lands of Machan and Cadzow were granted to one Walter Fitzgilbert. Fitzgilbert's family originated from Northumberland, and it is from this man that the Hamilton dynasty descended. Robert the Bruce had granted the lands to Walter Fitzgilbert for loyalty and service. The original grant of lands became divided between his descendents, resulting in three branches of the Hamilton family who would own most of Dalserf Parish and play an important part in the making of Scottish history, both at the local and government level. The three families (or septs) were the Dalserf Hamiltons, the Raploch Hamiltons and the Broomhill Hamiltons. The Dalserf Hamiltons' estate took in a great part of the Clyde Valley, including Dalserf Village. The Raploch Hamiltons' magnificent mansion stood on the site of the present St Marys church, while the Broomhill Hamiltons' estate overlooked the panoramic Avon Gorge.

This powerful dynasty also produced the Dukes of Hamilton, the Dukes of Chatelherault, the Earls of Arran and the Hamiltons of Craignethan Castle. The families deliberately retained the Hamilton name, whether the connection was by blood or through marriage, in order to take advantage of the protection offered by its power. Unfortunately for the local people, the high profile in national events maintained by their landed gentry resulted in the failure of the area to develop until the eighteenth century. Many of Larkhall's oldest street names have either a historical, religious or political connection, and a significant number are a direct result of the Hamilton families' input into the area. Their influence can be seen by the following names: Hamilton Street, Cadzow Street, Raploch Street, McNeil Street, Montgomery Street, Claude Street, Percy Street, Broomhill Road, Keir

Hardie Road and Robert Smillie Crescent. In the 1960s, when the seat was held by the Scottish Nationalist Party (SNP), a very Scottish theme emerged with names such as St Andrews Path, Wallace Drive, Bruce's Loan, and, of course, Bannockburn Wynd.

The Hamilton family was a staunch supporter of the monarchy through their connection of marriage to the Stewart dynasty and Roman Catholicism, later converting to the new reformed faith and adhering to it with the same zeal. In 1563, during the Reformation, a mob was on its way to the Castle of Auld Machan (seat of the Broomhill Hamiltons) with the intent to destroy the family's private place of worship, St Rhonans Chapel, or the Chapel Rone. Lady Elizabeth, wife of Sir John Hamilton, very bravely went outside and pleaded with them not to burn the sanctuary down. She promised: 'If ye dinnae burn it doon, I'll mak a good barn o'it'. She was as good as her word and the building stood until 1724, when it fell into ruins. The site of the former chapel lies on the site of the present day Broomhill Avenue, just beyond the now disused railway bridge.

The Hamilton families in the area suffered greatly because of their involvement with the ill-fated Mary Queen of Scots. Sir John Hamilton of Broomhill died of his wounds after Mary's final defeat at the Battle of Langside in 1568. His son Claude took flight to France. The Battle of Langside terminated Mary's cause in Scotland and she spent the remaining years of her tragic life being taken from one damp castle to another as the captured guest of her rival, Queen Elizabeth I, before being beheaded at Fotheringay Castle in 1587. On the orders of the Regent, James Stewart, Mary's illegitimate half-brother, an example was to be made of her supporters. Sir William Drury, Governor of Berwick, razed many Hamilton houses to the ground, including the castle of Auld Machan. Claude Hamilton of Broomhill returned three years later and Broomhill House was built on the foundations of the old castle. The Hamilton family again threw in their lot with the monarchy during the troubles that ultimately led to the execution of Charles I. Claude Hamilton supported the royalists in the Civil War and like his King perished on the scaffold at Whitehall. There is a path and wood near Millheugh in Larkhall called 'Mary Hozes'. This name is supposed to have originated from Mary Queen of Scots, who while fleeing from one Hamilton family to another was supposed to have rested in this wood and lost a stocking. The old Scots word for stocking was *hose*, hence from Mary's Hose to Mary Hozes.

The Parish of Dalserf was in the forefront of the Reformation, one of the most turbulent and bloody times in Scotland's history. The reformation lasted nearly a century and this area has always had a strong, religious background. Larkhall has a long-established connection with the Grand Orange Lodge of Scotland and has two Masonic lodges, much of which can be attributed to the large Irish population that settled in Scotland. Irish Catholics also settled, some fleeing the horrendous potato famine, and along with their Protestant counterparts mixed their own ideas and culture with that of the native Scots.

It is now at this part of the introduction that I would like to discuss the factors which advanced Larkhall as a town. The first and most dominant factor was the craft of the handloom weavers, a specialized occupation done in the light of their humble cottages. Many of the older streets in Larkhall were once weavers' cottages and have long since been modernized. A large proportion were the old single-ends like The Pleasances, Low Street and High Miller Street. In 1790, Larkhall had 100 looms, and in the 1840s, 462 weavers. This represented just under half the population of the town. The advancement of the Industrial Revolution and the invention of more advanced machinery began taking the weaving trade into mill and factory conditions. With the exception of forward thinking men such as David Dale and Robert Owen, who founded the New Lanark Mills, the conditions in most of these mills and factories were both hazardous and horrendous, with the workers receiving little reward for the long hours and conditions in which they worked. The handloom weavers working from home were fearful for their livelihood and the cottage weavers in Larkhall decided to form their own friendly societies, which implemented a rudimentary but effective form of health care.

Another development was the introduction of long leases allowing ordinary hard-working folk to own their own homes. It had a great effect on morale and from it the name 'the wee bonnet lairds' was born. In the period between 1880 and 1920, two-thirds of the population owned their own property, which was quite an achievement for such a small town. The next factor was the development of good, serviceable coach roads for travellers moving south to north, east to west and vice-versa. Larkhall had the London to Carlisle and Carlisle to Glasgow coach road running through it, and nearby at the River Clyde, the Garrion Bridge was built over the Edinburgh to Ayr coach road. The advent of coach roads led to an increase in the volume of people, livestock and goods that passed through the town and gave would-be settlers an idea of what it would be like to dwell and lay their roots there.

The advent of the steam engine also played its part in the area's prosperity. The Caledonian Railway Company came to Larkhall in 1856 with the building of the East Station in the north-east of the much expanding town. At first this was used as a goods station to shunt coal out of the town from the now numerous surrounding pits. The line also became a passenger line in 1868. The Central Station opened in 1905 on the other side of town and was used for both goods and passengers. The train contributed to the industrial growth of the town. It certainly helped to bring business investment to the area and gave the local inhabitants a better mobility to travel outwith the town in search of employment. Unfortunately, the line was hit like so many others by the Beeching cuts of the 1960s.

The very same year that the Central Station was opened in 1905 saw the arrival of another mode of transport in the tram. The company was Lanarkshire Tramway and Larkhall was route No.10. The Tramway Company by 1929 had changed its name to the Lanarkshire Traction Company and began to operate buses in the 1930s, eventually becoming the well-known SMT Company. Sadly, the last tram was withdrawn in Larkhall in 1928, but with names such as 'Charing Cross' and 'The Terminus', the memory of the tram lives on.

Larkhall was one of the first towns in Scotland to form its own co-operative society. The idea came from the early handloom weavers who had the basic principle that life could be made more comfortable and that hard work would be rewarded in a time when most working class families were well below the abject poverty line. The societies reverted back to the friendly society names of St Thomas Dalserf Insurance Militia (1802 or 1814), Masons Lodge (1823), The Millheugh and Larkhall Friendly

Society, The Larkhall Pleasance Building Society (1814), Larkhall Building Society (1824) and The Millheugh Building Society (1840). The Co-op proved to be a great asset, covering all basic human needs - food, clothing, footwear and medicine, and paid out a dividend to its members for their support. This dividend was often a boost to most families with wooden Co-op cheques to purchase.

The Victualling Society was formed in 1821. The original site was in Hamilton Street in Larkhall. By 1830 it had moved to Wellgate Street and then in 1894 to the red sandstone buildings in Union Street, now sadly demolished to make way for modern architecture.

The Montgomery Co-op was to follow this society. It was started by men of temperance and a group called 'The Good Shepherds', whose abhorrence to alcohol led to the motto 'neither, touch, taste or smell'. The Sons of Scotland, now Ansvar in Larkhall, originated from the above movement. The Scottish Co-operative Wholesale Society (SCWS) took over in 1961. Long gone are the days of the old Co-op book and the quaint way of serving someone on a one-to-one basis, with fast self-service stores now the order of the day. Many a Larkhall lad or lassie, including myself, has spent some of their working life employed by the Co-operative.

Perhaps the most crucial factor in the development of Larkhall was the discovery of the black diamonds. Larkhall was found, after study, to sit on rich coal seams, and coal mining arrived in the town at around the end of the eighteenth century with about four working pit sites. Miners' rows were often purposely built outside of a town with places such as Merryton Rows, Summerlee Rows, The Bog, and The Buffy all famous to Larkhall. Gradually, after years of hard work and endurance, improvements were made to the pits and things became better for the men known as 'Jock the Brutes'. One particular benefit was the nationalization of pits. This took the power away from the hands of the private pit owners like the Duke of Hamilton who mostly offered poor pay, bad housing and horrendous pit conditions without a trade union to argue the miners' case. My own father spent fifty-one years of his life in the pits at the coalface, suffering numerous injuries and on one occasion was trapped for almost two days. He died an agonising death, like so many of his fellow workers, with what was simply called 'Miners' Lung'. As his daughter, I hold his legacy with pride.

Larkhall folk have always been keen supporters of recreational pastimes. A football club, Larkhall Thistle, was formed in 1878 and is still active today. Famous football names such as the Gibsons, McLeans and McStays, have all become synonymous with Larkhall. There are two bowling greens and tennis and badminton courts for those interested in other sporting pursuits.

In the early twentieth century there was a music hall and then two cinemas, the Regal in Union Street and the Empire in King Street. The Empire is now a bingo hall. A lot of old-fashioned winching went on in the back seat when the lights went down! The Miners, Welfare Hall, built in the 1920s, had concerts on a Friday night, or 'geggies' as they were known locally. Social clubs like the British Legion and Larkhall Thistle Club still provide a focal point for the town's community to gather, while the Masonic Lodge and Orange Lodge organize their own events. Many a young man found his future wife at these social events. How apt was the saying: 'I met her at a wedding in the Co-operative Hall'.

'Larkie Fair' was held every year in Bryces Park in London Street and at one time it took two parks to stage the event. The Fair took place in June and was a much anticipated event for the old or young. I remember with affection walking with my parents and family with the smell of diesel and the atmosphere and noise of the fairground all around. You would often meet friendly folk or relations who would hand you whatever change they had in their pocket. This stretched the money a wee bit further and allowed you a few more goes on whatever took your fancy. Sometimes it meant another shot on the Stalls, which used to mean wining another goldfish to carry home in a plastic bag if you were lucky. Unfortunately, one of mine became my grandfather's cat's supper! The queue up London Street along Raploch Street to McMillans Fish and Chip Shop (now Tucks) on the way home was something else I recall about the Fair. The food, however, was well worth waiting for!

The yearly Gala Day was another focal point for the community. The Gala Day, with the multi-coloured floats and the people standing and waving, has encouraged a strong community spirit. The excited and radiant young Gala Queen with her attendants dressed in their regalia is a lovely sight and something that will live in the memories of these young girls for the rest of their lives.

Larkhall like all other towns exists, lives and regenerates itself through the people who make it. I have discussed the development of the town, but it certainly would have been a ghost town had it not been for the character and spirit displayed from its earliest natives to its most recent settlers. Larkhall has been known as a place of many characters and is well-known to such an extent that an imaginary wall is said to have been built around the town, perhaps created by outsiders, or maybe even by ourselves. Larkhall, due to the present climate, has its fair share of problems, but we are no worse or no better off than other contemporary towns. The reputation given to it as a rather narrow-minded and religiously biased place to live is quite unjustified, certainly in today's society. The folk that you meet as you stroll around the town are friendly and pleasant, with the old close-knit village syndrome still quite apparent. Years ago it was jokingly said that everyone in Larkhall was connected through the Co-operative horse or the Co-operative book!

Larkhall has always been known as a modern and forward-thinking town. We have a history going back many centuries to be proud of, and whatever your origins, if you live in Larkhall you are part of it. The town will go on and the stories of Harry Dawson and others will be carried into the next century. After all, folklore only gets better with age!

One

A Walk Around Larkhall

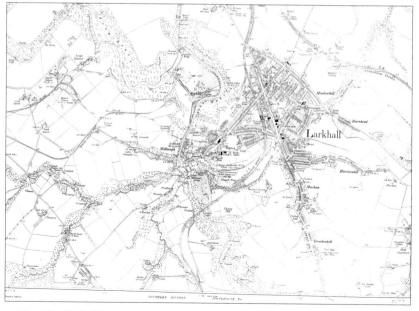

Map of Larkhall, 1913.

Larkhall Cross, *c*.1890. This is Larkhall Cross looking up from London Street. Notice the dirt roads and wide pavements.

Larkhall main street, 1902. The bunting and the flags commemorate the coronation of Edward VII.

Larkhall in 1900. Laying pavements on the Machan Brae. The wall and gate on the left-hand side of the photograph was once an entrance to St Machan's church manse. The pit you see on the right-hand side is the Broomhill Colliery No.3 or the 'Juck' pit.

Larkhall Cross, c. 1870. Like all towns and villages the Cross seemed to be a meeting place where folk stood and chatted, especially the menfolk. Notice the finger posts now on the side of a later building.

Union Street, Larkhall, c.1890. The small thatched cottage sits on the right-hand side, just in front of the man sitting on the horse and cart, and conceals the opening to Montgomery Street. Notice the telegraph pole on the right-hand side.

This thatched cottage stood in London Street. The name above the door is J. Galloway, Wines and Spirits, The Village Tavern. This depicts how pubs originated in Larkhall from small cottages such as this. The Village Tavern, though not in this site, still exists in London Street today.

Machan Road, Larkhall, *c*.1880. This thatched cottage illustrates the environment that those early weavers would work from.

This view is taken from Machan Road looking down into the town. In the distance you can see St Machan's church spire, and behind, Chalmers church spire, which was razed and rebuilt in the 1960s. Looking at this picture one can easily visualize those early coaches carrying weary travellers, trundling down the road.

Church Street, Larkhall. looking down towards Union Street around the turn of the twentieth century. The narrow road was widened upon the arrival of the tram in 1905.

Millheugh in Larkhall, c.1890. Millheugh was once a small separate hamlet that has long since been encompassed by Larkhall. It is a picturesque place nestling beside the River Avon.

This photograph was taken from the Stonehouse side of the River Avon, looking across Millheugh and up into Larkhall, illustrating the height at which Larkhall sits. Notice the large and splendid mansion on the right-hand corner of the photograph. The mansion is Broomhill House, seat of the Broomhill Hamiltons, which at that time was occupied by the McNeil-Hamiltons.

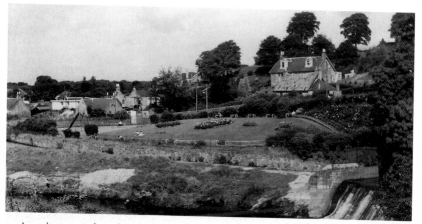

A much more modern photograph of Millheugh taken in the 1960s. Millheugh was often visited by Sunday school trips and families outwith Larkhall who wanted to picnic and enjoy the scenery and tranquility. It was known for Glasgow folk to take the tram just to spend a day at Millheugh and swim in the Avon. There are so many new houses and it is much changed which has altered its old world charm to a large degree.

Larkhall looking north, c.1950. This aerial photograph was taken by Guy Rodger of Larkhall from the top of Trinity church.

Larkhall looking south, taken from the same position. The left-hand side of the photograph shows what was part of Larkhall Academy in the 1960s. Next to the school building are three churches. From left to right they are: Chalmers church, the Congregational church and St Machan's.

Larkhall looking east.

Larkhall looking west. Notice on the right the Empire cinema. On the left is the Central Station, Raploch Bowling Club and beyond, the Gasworks football park.

Millheugh, looking towards the new bridge.

Trinity church just after its completion at the turn of the century. The church stands in Larkhall's Union Street.

Trinity church during its construction in the late 1890s – a great feat of architecture and achievement by the men who designed and built it. The stone being built into the wall was a commemorative plaque with a time capsule placed behind it. The men responsible for building it had to have a good head for heights and little thought for personal safety!

St Machan's church in Larkhall, pre-1922. St Machan's has been the parish church for the town since the mid-1850s.

The dedication of the church war memorial inside the grounds of St Machan's, 1921.

Inside Trinity church just after its completion in June 1901. The photograph is taken from the altar looking back. The church prior to this was in Wellgate Street in what is now St Thomas' Masonic Lodge. The total cost of the new building was £7,512 12s 1d.

The inside of Trinity church after its completion in 1901, looking towards the altar.

The inside of St Machan's church prior to its completion in the mid-1850s.

The Avon Gorge, part of which runs through Larkhall.

This photograph is of the old stone bridge at Millheugh, looking from the Morgan Glen side. The bridge was built in 1790 and even collapsed one night in 1934. Thankfully, no one was injured.

The new Millheugh Bridge, built in 1935 to replace the old stone bridge.

Union Street, Larkhall, around the late 1940s. Notice the Co-operative buildings on the left and the Trinity church and Regal cinema further down.

This modern photograph is taken from slightly further up Union Street, looking down towards London Street. The wee cottages on the left-hand side have gone and now shops take their place.

Present-day Union Street.

Church Street, Larkhall, 1920s –1930s. Note the small cottage with a shop attached.

Braehead Avenue takes its name from the Revd John McMillan, who was known as the Covenantor of Covenantors. His home of Braehead House stood on what is now Braehead Avenue. A small replica of his church, which was attached to his house, once stood in Millheugh Park. It was called "Tom Thumbs'" house by the locals.

Millheugh Brae, taken in the 1940s. The bottom of Millheugh Brae has changed much since earlier photographs. Many new bungalows now stand on this site now.

The old bridge at 'Mary Hozes' near Millheugh, Larkhall. The wood takes its name from Mary Queen of Scots, who as legend has it was supposed to have lost a stocking in the wood (see introduction). The bridge crosses the River Avon onto the Fairholm-Hamilton Estate and was nicknamed the 'bouncy bridge' by locals.

Broomhill House. Broomhill House was the once magnificent seat of the Broomhill Hamiltons, whose pedigree dates back to the Stewart throne. The house was built on the foundations of Auld Machan Castle, destroyed after the Battle of Langside in 1568.

The gatehouse to the Stevenson-Hamilton Estate, Larkhall. This family are a branch of the Broomhill/Raploch Hamiltons, who live in Fairholm House and play an active part in community life.

Right: Fairholm Lodge, belonging to the Stevenson-Hamilton Estate.

Below: Broomhill House, c.1910, looking up from the old bridge at Millheugh. The house has been rebuilt and modified over many centuries. Broomhill, already in a state of disrepair, caught fire in September 1943.

The gates to the Broomhill Estate. The long tree-lined avenue ran from these gates to Broomhill House, with the gatehouse sitting on the left-hand side of the photograph. My family has a long association with the estate and my grandmother Helen Perrie (nee Henderson) worked for seventy years with the family. My father's folk also worked and lived on the estate, both at the Home Farm and the gatehouse

Memorial Park, London Street. The picture has been taken looking towards the cenotaph. The cenotaph was erected in 1921 by public conscription.

An earlier photograph of Memorial Park, London Street.

This photograph shows Machanhill Primary School. The name of the school comes from the association with St Machan (see introduction). Machanhill was reputed to be one of the best teaching schools in Larkhall.

The unveiling of the War Memorial by the town dignitaries in the park on Sunday 30 October 1921. The local town folk look on.

The old stone bridge at Millheugh, c.1910, looking towards the Stonehouse side of the River Avon. Notice the hump on the bridge. – no 70mph traffic in those days!

A house at Canderside Toll, No. 51 Carlisle Road, 1905. Carlisle Road was the Larkhall to Glasgow and Carlisle to London coach road. The occupants in the picture are Mrs Brown and her family.

Millheugh, looking towards the old bridge.

This photograph is testament to the popularity of Millheugh in Larkhall. Look at all the happy expressions on the faces of the folk milling about in the river and standing on the rocks.

38

Millheugh, taken from the Clove Mill, with Larkhall sitting above, high on the hill. The chimney stack of the Bleachfield Cotton Works looms up into the sky.

Clove Mill Bridge, near Millheugh. Millheugh was also known as 'Spice Mill', a hive of industry for many decades in the eighteenth century.

The other side of the River Avon, looking from Larkhall to Millheugh.

GARRION BRIDGE, NEAR LARKHALL.

The Garrion Bridge was built to cross the River Clyde in the eighteenth century and remains unchanged except for the toll house on the left-hand side, which is now long-gone.

The Garrion Bridge and the toll house built on it. Trams used to stop at one point in time and tea was served to passengers. How different from today!

Old Hareleeshill. Most of these old homes were weavers' cottages. Many more modern district council and private development housing schemes have long since filled the rolling fields that you see in here.

Raploch Street, looking up towards the cross and across to Wellgate St, c.1890. Larkhall has always had the reputation for many years of having an abundance of good shops.

Raploch Street looking up to the Cross with the corner of McNeil Street on the right-hand side. A much later photograph, taken in the 1960s. On the right-hand corner sits the Victory Bar.

Braehead House in Millheugh, the site of the house and church of the Revd John McMillan, the 'Covenantor of Covenantors'. His church was the first of the reformed faith in Larkhall

JUBILEE LARKHALL CONGREGATIONAL CHURCH 1875-1925

The altar of the Congregational church in Larkhall. The church was built in 1875 and the photograph was taken to celebrate its jubilee in 1925.

The old parish church in Dalserf village on the River Clyde. The church was built in 1655 and is recognised as the mother church of the reformed faith (see introduction) in this area. The church still has a healthy and dedicated congregation and has been gifted with equally dedicated ministers from its beginnings to the present day. The church has two open days a year in May and September and is truly worth a visit. Its peaceful tranquillity whilst sitting in the old historical church is something to experience.

This curious picture is of a stone plaque once embedded in a house in Millheugh. It was known as the 'Adam and Eve' plaque and was taken from the old Plotcock Castle near Larkhall, which belonged to the Hamilton family.

Two

Transport

Union Street, *c.*1910. A tram is approaching Larkhall Cross in the distance.

The Cross, 1905, showing the single-track tramline entering the town and the double-track loop which ran through it.

Church Street, looking towards Union Street. The tram has just stopped at The Terminus, the last stop before the tram turned back through town and headed towards Glasgow. Names such as 'The Terminus,' 'Charing Cross' and 'The Cross' are spoken by Larkhall folk as a point of reference to modern day bus drivers.

Hamilton Road, Larkhall. Taken in the 1930s, the tramlines entering Larkhall from Hamilton, Uddingston and Glasgow are clearly visible. The Hamilton District Council housing scheme is also shown.

Trams at Larkhall Cross, 1910. The trams entering and leaving Larkhall are magnificent. Sitting on top of an open tram must have been quite an experience, but maybe not so pleasant on a wet and windy day!

Another shot of the tram at Larkhall Cross in 1910. The trams first came to Larkhall in 1905. The company was named 'Lanarkshire Tramways' and Larkhall was route No. 10. In 1929 the name was changed to the Lanarkshire Traction Company and by this time the new innovation was the bus. The last tram in Larkhall ran in 1928 and the lines were lifted in the 1930s.

Larkhall Cross, 1910, taken from further down London Street. From 1905 the tram and the train helped the growth of the town and gave locals the freedom to travel for social reasons and the ability to find work further afield.

The corner of Union and Church Streets. The tramlines are visible and just slightly further up on the left of the photograph, outside St Machan's parish church, was the Charing Cross tram stop.

Central Station in Larkhall, situated on Caledonian Road. The street was named after the Caledonian Railway Company, who built the line. The station was opened in 1905 and won first prize for 'best kept station' three years in a row. Unfortunately, the station closed in October 1965, when the line was hit by Dr Beeching's cuts. The station buildings were demolished in 1968 and the service has been very much missed since.

The Larkhall Viaduct before its opening in 1905. The engines you can see in the photograph were taken over the bridge on the line's Board of Trade Inspection to test for any flaws. Too bad for the men on the bridge if there had been!

King Street, looking towards the entrance to Central Station in Caledonian Road. The photograph was taken in 1905 when the station opened. King Street was constructed to help with access to the station.

The East Station in Larkhall. The station and railway line were first used for goods in 1856, changing to a passenger line in 1868.

Larkhall Viaduct. The viaduct, the highest in Scotland, is 170 ft high from ground level to the rail tracks. The viaduct, which towers majestically over the Morgan Glen, carried the railway line to Stonehouse, Strathaven and beyond. The bridge was built by the Arrol Bros of Glasgow.

This photograph shows the new bridge at Millheugh and the viaduct towering in the distance.

Three

Men in Uniform

A very early Larkhall fire brigade, c.1890. The picture was taken at the old police/fire station at Crossgates. The men served as policemen and firemen, combining just one pay for both occupations.

Here, the fire brigade is testing their equipment at the council chambers in Victoria Street. The photograph is dated 1896.

A later fire brigade, taken at the fire station when it was at Caledonian Road next to the police station. They were first motorized fire brigade in Larkhall.

Larkhall Fire Brigade in 1910. These men look very proud of their profession and rightly so.

Men from this parish have served their country loyally in all conflicts throughout the globe. The local regiment was The Cameronian Scottish Rifles, with Larkhall housing the 4th Battalion. Pictured here are some of the men prior to the Boer War at the turn of the twentieth century.

Four

Industry

The Silk Factory in Miller Street, Larkhall. Notice how little regard there was to personal safety. The lady in this photograph is Janet Brown, who went on to become Mrs Janet Rodger. The Rodgers' reputation as plumbers in Larkhall for service, standard and quality was second to none.

Farming in the area. The Dalserf Parish was very green and fertile and excellent for agriculture. The changes in farming came quickly with the idea of crop rotation, and consequently this area had some of the best farms in Scotland for quality of produce

Farming implement, c.1960.

Coal carters were independent businessmen who formed their own business and sub contracted to the pit, both with private owners and the NCB when the pits were nationalized. Famous names in Larkhall include Jackson Pringle.

The Merrytown Rows, Lanark Road End. The photograph depicts typical miners' rows. It was here that the famous Harry Dawson was born.

The Bleachfields at Millheugh, often referred to as the 'Avonbanks Works'. The Bleachfields were originally a whisky distillery in the mid-eighteenth century, before the boom of the Industrial Revolution. The works are no longer in existence.

The bottom of Millheugh Brae is shown here, along with the proximity of the Avonbanks Works to the Bleachfields.

Notice the man-made lake which was used to feed the works with water from the River Avon.

The Bleachfields, looking from the other side of the River Avon. This side of the river belonged to the Duke of Hamilton and was known as 'The High Parks'. It was where the famous white cattle were kept.

This photograph again shows the Bleachfields and the bottom of Millheugh Brae. The other side of the river shows the wood known as 'Mary Hozes', which leads to 'The High Parks.' The Stevenson-Hamilton estate lies on the other side of the river.

The Stonehouse side of the River Avon, looking across Millheugh. Notice the chimney stack belonging to the Bleachfields.

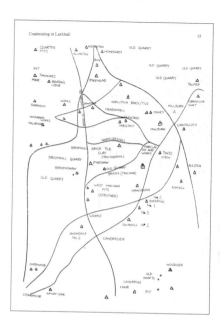

This map shows the number of viable pits working in this area prior to the 1940s.

George Paton is seen standing at the back with his wife and grandaughter (his father is sitting). George Paton was a well-respected manager of the Montgomery Society for many years.

THE LAIRDS O' LARKIE

'Wa back in auchteen seventeen,
When working folk were no' so bien,
A wheen o' weavers a' were fain
to own a wee hoose o' their ain.
Sae gethered the gither, ower a crack
Decided they wad ne'er look back
Till ilka wabster, ane an' a',
Were a' wee lairds o' Laverockha'.

Officials ap'inted, a' withoot fee,
A weaver's shop hoosed the comytee,
A modest loan at twa per cent,
Tae pey aff aland wi' rent.
'Twas thus the Ba' was set a -rowin'-
Till this day it's still a-growin'-
Frae this bit seedling gey an' sma'
Sprang up the lairdie Laverockha'.

At the Pleasance, owre the mair,
A site was foun' that promised fair,
An' there, in due course of time,
Arose that thing o' stane an' lime
To mark the first garden city plot,
A monument to a thrifty lot.
Letchworth, Port Sunlight, in fact them a'
Jist followed the lead o' Laverockha'.

Langsyne a humble but an' ben
Sufficed even kings o' men,
But noo a cot we' roomies twa
Is considered no' the thing ava:
A self-contained, gairden, front an' back,
A scullery an' bathroom they winna lack,
Bedrooms and parlours, it tak's them a'
To please new lairds o' Laverockha'.

Above: The Montgomery Society with a stall in an unknown Larkhall location. Third from the left is Mr George Paton, the manager. The sign reads SCWS, which stood for Scottish Co-operative Wholesale Society.

Left: This poem was written in honour of those early weavers and their forward thinking ideas and principles, from which arose the saying the 'Lairds O' Larkie, the wee bonnet lairds.' The author is unknown.

Five

Gala Day

Gala Day, 1950s. Larkhall like so many other towns and villages had its annual Gala Day with the crowning of the Gala Queen and the many events that precipitated. The Gala was well supported by the local folk and businesses. There was a great Cinderella feeling for the local girl picked to be the queen and it was an equally exciting day for her attendants.

The people line the main street.

Looking down Wellgate Street on Gala Day. The man standing at the window in a building on the left was Mr Rodger, a dentist in Larkhall for many years.

The corner of McNeil Street between Church Street and Union Street on a 1950s Gala Day. The Co-op supplied the float on this occasion.

This photograph is taken at nearly the same spot. The 65 'special' is coming down the line.

Union Street during a gala day in the 1950s. Larkhall had a sizeable movement of Boy Scouts, Cubs and Lifebuoys.

The building on the left is the Victualling Co-operative Society. The town band is leading the gala queen and her attendants' cortege.

Gala Queen Agnes Jackson being piped into Morgan Glen, 1953. Morgan Glen was once part of Broomhill Estate and the queen, for many years, was crowned here.

The 1953 Gala Queen preparing to be photographed for the local newspaper, the *Hamilton Advertiser*.

The crowning of Agnes Jackson by her predecessor. This scene is a perfect illustration of the amount of preparation that went into the crowning ceremony of the queen on Gala Day.

The Gala Queen of 1954, again taken in Morgan Glen.

The Gala Queen of 1954 during her crowning ceremony. Unfortunately, the Gala Day, as such, is now non-existent.

The open-air bandstand and small stadium where the Gala Queen was crowned in Morgan Glen. The River Avon runs through Morgan Glen and part of the 'Glen' was once Broomhill Estate. Morgan Glen runs from Birkenshaw to Strutherhill and down to Millheugh. Dances and concerts used to be held on a regular basis in the bandstand, which is now sadly gone. Morgan Glen lies in the middle of the panoramic Avon Gorge.

The bandstand and stadium again. The trees and greenery are very much Morgan Glen and are part of the Broomhill Estate in Millheugh.

The 1953 Gala Queen after her crowning ceremony.

A little girl dressed up in costume during a 1950 gala at Morgan Glen. The Larkhall Viaduct is in the background.

May Queen and Attendants, Larkhall May-Day Festival 1921.

The Larkhall May Queen and her attendants in 1921 on May Day. May Day was a celebration created by the working class to commemorate their struggle against injustice. It was also known as Labour Day.

LARKIE FAIR

Air.—"The Happy Days of Youth"
"Twas on a smiling morn in June, it being Larkie Fair,
And having rowth of leisure-time, I sauntered awa 'there;
The sun was shining bonnie an' the lark was singing fine,
Tou'd thocht a blessing dwelt on a' for auld langsyne."

BONNIE LARKHA!

Sweet spot o' my childhood, my birth-place, my pride,
That tranquilly lies o'erlooking the Clyde,
'Mid scenes o' fresh beauty the sweetest o' a',
My ain native village o' bonnie Larkha'.

The laverock at heaven's yett abune thee sings sweet
Its sang o' blithe joy the bright mornin' tae greet,
Wi' merles gay chanting an' peewit's weird ca',
To me thou art dearer O bonnie Larkha'.

The ripe fields aroon thee are fair tae behold,
An' gae back their treasures to thee manifold,
Awaiting blithe reapers fu' ripe for the fa',
Bringing cheer tae the cotters o' bonnie Larkha'.

Surrounded wi' beauty that's hard tae compare,
The rarest o' orchards to view everywhere,
An' wi' Avon's sweet vale, the fairest o' a',
Thou art sweetly enhanced O bonnie Larkha'.

I cherish thy freenship whaur loving hearts beat,
I hallow they memories tae me ever sweet,
Nae spot that I ken or in truth can I ca',
Half sae dear tae my heart as bonnie Larkha'.

This poem was written by an unknown author, describing how he and his fellow townsfolk felt about Larkhall. It is entitled *Bonnie Larkha*.

Six

Do You Recognise Anyone?

Hugh McIntyre's butchers shop, Wellgate Street, 1933. From left to right: Miss McIntyre, G. Allan, W. Perrie and Nat Thompson.

Larkhall Leisure Centre just after the swimming baths were built. The commemoration stone was laid by Miss Mary McLaughlin. Standing on the left of this lady was a JP (Justice of the Peace) and a stalwart of the Labour Party from its early days.

At play in Robert Smillie Park, 1950. In the background is the Strutherhill housing scheme. The park is still very much in use but the little train has long gone. Part of the park belonged to the Broomhill Hamilton Estate and another part formed a long tree-lined avenue.

In the background lies the entrance to Robert Smillie Park. The round turrets were once the gates to the Broomhill Hamilton Estate.

Enjoy the ride!

A well-known Larkhall couple 'courting'. The lady is Janet Rodger (*née* Brown) and her future husband is Mr Robert Rodger. This was the first car in Larkhall, driven by owner John MacLachlan, uncle of Mr Rodger.

Mr George Allan, another businessman who owned a butchers shop in Wellgate Street.

The wife of the above Mr Allan, 1900. Her maiden name was Isabella Kerr.

This photograph shows the children of Mr and Mrs Allan in 1912.

Andrew Allan, as a baby in 1912. Notice the style of buggy - how ideas go round in cycles! Andrew claims he was the fattest baby in Larkhall. He certainly looks healthy and is still an alert man, even in his eighties!

The Larkhall Camera Club during its first outing, 1901. See if you can fill in the gaps. The chap sitting on the far right-hand side is Mr Robert Rodger, while alongside him sits Mr Mathew McWhirter, another Larkhall legend in the political field. An eventide home is named after this gentleman in Larkhall, the Mathew McWhirter Home, in Raploch Street.

The Camera Club at a social function in 1922. The photograph was taken in the Clydesdale Masonic Lodge in Larkhall.

Some of the members of the Larkhall Camera Club pose for a picture of their own in the 1920's.
Mr R. Milligan, on the far right of the picture, was the sanitary inspector for many years in this area.

The Larkhall Camera Club outside the Popinjay Hotel in the Clyde Valley, 1920.

The 'coming of age' of the Camera Club in 1922 (twenty-one years). This photograph of the old bridge at Millheugh was printed on the front of the social function card.

A Larkhall Scout Troup.

Above: The Larkhall Scout Pipe Band taken outside the Empire cinema. The Scout movement was seen as a great idea for young boys and young men. The movement encouraged friendship, a strict code of conduct and gave these young lads something to look forward to through meetings and the wonderful experience of going away to Scout camp.

Left: Rug-making was quite an art.

Miss McNeish who had a drapers shop in Wellgate Street.

Mrs Allan (*née* Kerr), whose husband had a butchers shop in Wellgate Street. The other lady is her grandmother, Helen Kerr. Note the style of dress common in the Edwardian era.

Above: A 1920s school photograph, which highlights the style of clothing and reminds us of the format used for many years when class photographs were taken.

Left: Captain Henry Montgomery McNeil-Hamilton of Raploch and Broomhill, and the last laird of that ilk. He was born in 1872 and died in 1924, having lived at Broomhill, the seat of the Broomhill Hamiltons, for many centuries. The gentleman was married to Edith Thompson Carmichael, daughter of another leading Scottish aristocratic family. The house no longer exists with only bits of stone and rubble to denote where it once stood.

Millburn Farm, c.1910. The younger gentleman on the right-hand side of the photograph is the famous impressionist painter, Hunter, who was one of the famous 'Glasgow Boys.'

Victualling Society Dance, 1940s. Everyone looks like they are having a great time!

The Larkhall Girls Brigade, c.1960s.

Trinty Church elders with their minister, 1952.

A series of old school photographs.

Two of the photographs were taken by J.A. Prophet of Shields Road, Glasgow. This company specialised in taking school photographs in and around Glasgow.

Machanhill Primary, c.1930.

Do you recognise yourself in any of these views?

90

Above: Larkhall Bowling Club, 1910. The president was Mr John Steel, father to Mr Andrew Steel (see below).

Right: Mr Andrew Steel, President of Larkhall Bowling Club (The Old Green), in 1968. Andrew Steel, like his father, was a well-known and much respected businessman in Larkhall for many years. Steel's shop stood at the corner of Montgomery Street and Union Street.

Mrs Steel receiving a presentation from Mr Miller, vice-president of Larkhall Bowling Club, 1968. Andrew Steel and Mrs Miller are also pictured.

Centenary directors and past presidents of Larkhall Bowling Club, 1968. In 1869 the club had fifty-six members and the subscription was 10s. The earliest bowl house seems to have been a hut and with the advancement of time a single-storey brick house was erected. Prior to this time the game of bowls was probably played at Crossgates.

Seven

Do You Remember These Businesses?

Lee the Baker, well-renowned for their Scotch mutton pies.

I am sure the fish and chips were delicious, but look at the amount of seated accomodation this restaurant catered for. Quite something for what was really a small village.

Many a caramel sweet I purchased here as a 'lassie.'

Many an ice cream I enjoyed from Capaldi's.

Larkhall folk like to socialise! On the whole, the town is a friendly place and has always had a number of places where people can 'pass the time of day' and enjoy a refreshment with one another. Berries Hotel was one such place.

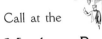

Left: Larkhall has many such meeting places that enjoy their fair share of regular clientele, particularly pubs like the Machan Bar!

Below: The Central Bar in Union Street was also known as The Maltings and had a function room at the back.

Daks Simpson's has been in Larkhall for many years, beginning in Miller Street in what used to be the old silk factory. Daks' gents suits have a global recognition for their quality and the factory has employed many Larkhall men and women over the years.

Larkhall has been noted for its vast number of shops, among them, The Clydesdale Hosiery Co. Ltd.

E. Hamilton

LADIES' OUTFITTER

•

98 Union Street LARKHALL

The variety within the clothing market in Larkhall was also evident. As well as this independent outlet there was also the Co-operative.

JAMES MOFFAT

Coat and Gown Specialist

69 Union Street, Larkhall

Telephone : Larkhall 101

No wonder Larkhall was considered a 'boom town', particularly when one had the luxury of visiting 'James Moffat, Coat and Gown Specialist.'

This shop had an old-world charm about it.

You could even get a fancy hairdo and just look at the
prices as compared with today.

Larkhall has always had a number of chemists, with Simpson's being an old established family business.

Bruce the chemist was also once a well-established family business. The daughter, Eva Bruce, carried on her father's business for many years.

WM. FRAME, JNR.

Garage and Filling Station

HAMILTON ROAD
LARKHALL

REPAIRS
PETROL
OIL
SPARES

Above: Not so many cars back then. We now have three filling stations in Larkhall.

Right: In addition to the car being filled with petrol, one could also purchase some Clyde Valley Tomatoes.

Telephone: Larkhall 27

CLYDE VALLEY FILLING STATION

for Petrol, Oils and Tyres, etc.

LANARK ROAD END
BY HAMILTON

Proprietor : WM. C. BLACKLEY

Clyde Valley Tomatoes

WILLIAM C. BLACKLEY

Lanark Road End, by Hamilton

Larkhall has enjoyed the 'best of both worlds' in days gone by and even still now with land which is great for growing crops, vegetables and fruit.

Larkhall sits in the middle of prime farming land, so our grain is of the highest standard.

DONALD MACKAY

Cooked Meat Specialist

Home - Fed BEEF
MUTTON & LAMB
at Lowest Market
Prices

ORDERS CALLED FOR
AND DELIVERED

Spiced Rounds, Pickled Tongues and Sausages a speciality
POULTRY AND EGGS DIRECT FROM FARM

88 UNION STREET, LARKHALL

'Healthy land' meant 'healthy livestock', typified by the popularity of butchers such as Donald Mackay.

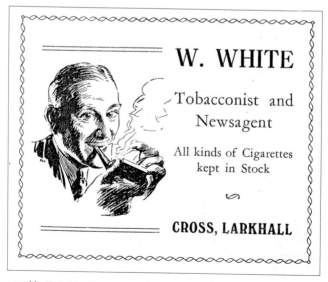

W. WHITE

Tobacconist and
Newsagent

All kinds of Cigarettes
kept in Stock

CROSS, LARKHALL

Tobacconists like W. White flourished in the days of Woodbines and cigarette cards.

Left: George B. Jamieson – not only a funeral undertaker, but also the first taxi service in Larkhall.

Below: This advertisement is for Andrew Dick, an earlier undertaker in Larkhall and the forerunner to the previous undertaker, George B. Jamieson. Larkhall now has two undertakers, the Co-op and Dorricot and Bent.

William Wilson, a 'jack of all trades', with joinery, building and funeral undertaking amongst the services that he provided.

Allan Thompson, another who believes in diversity!

Robert Rodger – Larkhall's famous plumber and gasfitter.

The 'coal connection' in Larkhall has been consistent throughout the town's history.

This advertisement is for William Prentice & Sons, another well-established family business renowned for their craftmanship and standard.

Even then, businesses such as R. M. Kirkwood were using popular slogans to advertise.

LARKHALL
AND DISTRICT'S
BEST
SHOPPING CENTRE

LARKHALL Co-operative Society is the *best* shopping centre of Larkhall and District. Visitors are welcome here, where they will receive first-class service and the highest quality of goods—S.C.W.S. PRODUCTIONS—at strictly competitive prices. Visitors and non-members are paid half dividend on all purchases. Goods will be promptly delivered to your door, so phone Larkhall 36, or call at the Larkhall Co-operative Store, 56 Montgomery Street. IT PAYS TO

SHOP AT THE CO-OP
AND ALWAYS ASK FOR
S.C.W.S. PRODUCTIONS

TELEPHONE	LARKHALL 36
Address: 56 MONTGOMERY ST., LARKHALL	

LARKHALL
CO-OPERATIVE SOCIETY LTD.

Page four

Old Co-op adverts.

BRITAIN'S FINEST FOOTWEAR

SHIELDHALL
FASHION-FIT FOOTWEAR

EASY ON THE FEET AND ON THE PURSE

HALL MARK — SCWS

THIS MARK IS STAMPED ON THE SOLE

LATEST DESIGNS | BEST QUALITY | KEENEST PRICES

Manufactured by the Scottish Co-operative Wholesale Society Limited, Shieldhall— and sold at the Boot Department of the

LARKHALL
CO-OPERATIVE SOCIETY LTD.

Page five

Eight

Another Walk Around Larkhall

Muir Street, looking towards Union Street, late nineteenth century. To the left, is the 'Low and High Pleasance' building, their name coming from the Larkhall Pleasance Building Society that was formed in 1814. These building societies originated from the forward thinking domestic weavers known as the 'wee bonnet lairds.'

Machan Road, c.1905. Along from the large hedgerows where a petrol filling station is now situated, was a once thriving pit – ironically close to the prestigious houses on the other side. The pit was nicknamed the 'Juck' due to a water problem. The 'Kitchen' burn now runs through what was once the pit, with bungalows and other homes built around the surrounding area.

Hamilton Road Junction, meeting London Street. The photograph dates from the 1920s and remains virtually unchanged.

The old Larkhall Academy. Once known as the 'new academy' or the 'red building', because of its beautiful red sandstone brick. This lovely building was opened in 1896, largely due to a growth in the town's population. Now sadly demolished, the present Larkhall Academy is situated on what was once part of the Hamiltons' Broomhill Estate

Trinity church in Union Street, not long after its completion and opening in 1901.

Larkhall Cross, looking down Wellgate Street. The old Cross used to be situated at the corner of Drygate, where Drygate and Hamilton Street meet. This was the route the earlier travellers would have used passing through Larkhall when Drygate formed part of the Ayr to Edinburgh road in 1791. The new route through Larkhall arose in 1819, with Union Street, Church Street and London Street becoming the main streets one would pass through. The new Cross is at the corner of Union Street and Raploch Street. On the other side, Union Street and Wellgate Street corner passed on into London Street, and then on out of the town.

Larkhall Cross, c.1910, looking up from London Street. Notice the folk 'milling about' and the tramlines. The Cross is still very much the same today.

This photograph of Millheugh and the River Avon illustrates how peaceful and beautiful the village once was. A ferry crossed the river at this point prior to 1790.

Millheugh, looking from the opposite side of the river. Notice the lade into the Bleachfield Cotton Works.

Looking towards the old bridge at Millheugh with the viaduct in the distance.

A train speeds along the highest viaduct in Scotland, offering a breathtaking view.

The Ayr Road branch of the Victualling Society. The whiteness of the aprons is a good advert for old-fashioned soap powder.

Fairholm House. The house is situated on the Fairholm Estate on the opposite side of the River Avon from Millheugh and belonged to the Stevenson-Hamilton family, descendants of the Raploch and Broomhill Hamiltons.

The old bridge at Millheugh and Broomhill House.

The once opulent Hamilton Palace, situated in nearby Hamilton. This was the home of the Dukes of Hamilton, descendants from the Broomhill Hamiltons. The palace had been in existence since 1591 with alterations, of course, over many decades. Surprisingly, this magnificent buliding remained unscathed during some of Scotland's most bloody and turbulent periods in history. James Hamilton, second Earl of Arran, was the instigator of the original building. The palace, like so many other fine palaces and castles, came to a rather sad end with crippling death duties. These affected a lot of aristocratic families who were forced to abandon their huge homes due to the astronomical cost of maintaining them. The Hamilton family left the palace in 1916 and moved to Dungavel Lodge near Strathaven, with the demolition beginning in 1922. The family then moved onto Lennoxlove, near Haddington, in 1972.

This photograph was taken in the park at Millheugh, a beautiful park with lovely displays of floral beds. This one is in the shape of a clock.

The entrance to Robert Smillie Park. Robert Smillie, who once lived in Miller Street, was a stalwart in the early Labour Party. Hailing from Ireland, Smillie was a dynamic thinker who worked earnestly to improve conditions for the working class, particularly the miners. Robert Smillie Crescent is named in his honour. In the distance is the new Larkhall Academy and on the right-hand side is the new Larkhall Leisure Centre.

The entrance into Morgan Glen from Millheugh. Morgan Glen takes its name from Captain Morgan, a retired sea captain who owned the Applebank Inn in Millheugh in the mid-eighteenth century. Captain Morgan purchased the land from the Broomhill Hamilton Estate and gifted it to the people of Larkhall for recreational purposes. The 'Glen', with the River Avon running through it, is a lovely place to walk and has proved very popular with families and courting couples! South Lanarkshie Council is now responsible for its upkeep.

Above: The Applebank Inn in Millheugh. A lovely old pub which has retained much of its charm. The inn originates from 1714 when it was an alehouse and is still a busy and bustling pub with excellent food and great hospitality. The pub even has its own ghost, 'The Black Lady.'

Right: Cathy and Alan Chalmers, the owners of the Applebank Inn.

Inside the Applebank Inn. The large piece of stone in the photograph is the lintel taken from Broomhill House and placed in the Applebank during the 1960s. This explains the connection between the Applebank and the ghost of 'The Black Lady', a mysterious Leylon woman who lived at Broomhill House.

ON THE AVON, LARKHALL

Above: The old bridge at Millheugh, taken from the Morgan Glen side.

Right: Dalserf church, which lies nestling beside the River Clyde in the beautiful Clyde Valley.

The bottom of present day Millheugh Brae. So many changes have occurred here.

The Clove Mill Bridge near Millheugh.

Patrickholm, situated on the Stonehouse side of the River Avon and part of the large Hamilton Estate. Notice the crest above the door.

The corner of Raploch Street, Morgan Street and Raploch Road. A baker by the name of Peter Gordon once owned the shop on the corner. It is now the office of one of the local taxi firms, LTOA.

The new fire station in Claude Street. Prior to this it was situated in Caledonian Street, next to the police station.

Chatelherault, near Larkhall. Chatelherault was once the hunting lodge of the Dukes of Hamilton. Work began in 1732 under the orders of James V, Duke of Hamilton, and was completed in 1744. The name comes from their French title, the Dukes of Chatelherault.

The inside of the Baptist church prior to its completion in 1964.

Chalmers Church, Strutherhill. Previously, the old church was situated in Union Street in Larkhall.

CENTENARY

St. Mary's, Larkhall

CELEBRATION

1872 ——— *Souvenir Brochure* ——— 1972

Above: Another photograph of Chalmers Church. The new church was opened in the 1950s. The congregation is led by Mr Hastie.

Left: St Mary's Roman Catholic church. The church is situated in what was once the Raploch Hamilton Estate. In 1872 a chapel school was built and in 1905 the new church was opened. A Roman Catholic mission was established in Hamilton in 1846 and mass was said in Larkhall for the first time in Scanlon's Hotel in Raploch Street. Cannon McGinn leads the St Mary's congregation.

Larkhall Raploch Bowling Club, 1987. The Raploch Bowling Club was formed in 1982, taking over from the Larkhall Miners Welfare when it closed in 1981.

Larkhall Raploch Bowling Club, 1994. The club has 200 male members and 120 female members. The club has been very successful in tournaments in both the ladies and gentlemens section. It also has a junior section encouraging younger members to get involved and enjoy the game. This photograph was taken at Dalserf Bowling Club when Raploch won the Lanarkshire Top.

Inside Raploch Bowling Club, 1994. The three gentlemen enjoying a 'wee dram' are left to right: W. Jamieson, J. Cook and D. Leggate. Enjoy it lads!